# DECOMPOSITION

# DECOMPOSITION

*An Anthology of Fungi-Inspired Poems*

*edited by*

Renée Roehl *&* Kelly Chadwick

LOST HORSE PRESS
Sandpoint · Idaho

# ACKNOWLEDGEMENTS

Innumerable people touched this project. It was a community affair.

First and foremost we are at a loss of words for Sam Ligon. Without his profound involvement, this project would never have gone farther than one of many pipe dreams. He provided the initial encouragement, and worked with us reading, selecting, offering editing advice, and much more.

We are deeply appreciative for Brett Ortler of *Knockout Literary Magazine* who supplied numerous leads, contact information, procedural advice and support. His religious service to poetry will continue to expand the growing web of verse to the benefit of us all.

For help in the discovery of content, we are grateful to David Rose, Maggie Rogers, Moselio Schaechter and Elizabeth Dodd.

For assistance contacting the many contributors, we thank Christopher Howell and David Chadwick whose threads through fifty years of counter-culture were critically helpful. From the next two generations, we thank Tom Holmes and Jonathan Johnson.

With publishing and marketing advice, Michael Katz and Michael J. Rosen kindly guided us through naïve ambiguity.

And lastly to our many friends who listened as we read countless poems—whether they wanted to or not—in our kitchen, on road trips, at parties. Most of all to our son, Dario Ré, with his artistic sensibility and inquisitive mind; Ron Brock, with his unfailing clarity of opinion; and Drew Parker, with his patience and advice throughout the project.

Cover Art: "Magic Mushrooms" by Kim Dunn Murphy
Editors' Photo: Dario Ré
Book & Cover Design: Christine Holbert

This and other LOST HORSE PRESS titles may be viewed online at www.losthorsepress.org.

FIRST EDITION

LIBRARY OF CONGRESS CATALOGING-IN-PUBLICATION DATA

Decomposition : fungi-inspired poetry / edited by Kelly Chadwick & Renée Roehl.
        p. cm.
ISBN 978-0-9844510-0-5 (alk. paper)
1. Fungi—Poetry. 2. American poetry—21st century. I. Chadwick, Kelly, 1973- II. Roehl, Renée, 1953-
PS615.D43 2010
811'.608—dc22

                    2010004760

# CONTENTS

## VEIL

## FRUITING BODY

# RUIN · COLLAPSE

# FORWARD

The mushrooms that appear in these pages are named erotic, secretive, deconstructive, ephemeral. They are graspable carriers of transformation, ground-murmurers of both death and birth, embodiments of wildness, modesty, danger, hope. With an infrequency somewhat surprising, they are cooked, eaten. The shape of prayer appears in these poems almost as often as the shape of the phallus. Knuckles and ears also recur.

Yet the varieties of mushroom-description are as boundless as fungi themselves. In a single line, Marvin Bell names them caps, hairdos, mini-umbrellas, and zeppelins. Margaret Atwood compares them to red balloons, the thumbs of inverted rubber gloves, parallel thunderstorms struck from the earth. Robert Bly finds the tough, cracking heel of a foot and the faces of travelers. For Emily Dickinson, mushrooms are Nature's Apostates, for David Young they are doorknobs to darkness, for Robert Penn Warren, basketable stars. Arthur Sze recognizes in mushrooms his own passions "mycorrhizal with nature." Sylvia Plath and Ann Lauinger each offers herself as fungal medium: mushrooms speak through them to us in first person address.

Writing of mushrooms, it seems, can bring out the rarely seen in a poet. This collection holds a poem by Gary Snyder in rhymed quatrains, and one of the only love poems Elizabeth Bishop published during her lifetime. Not only mushrooms but other members of the third kingdom appear here—Bishop's poem describes the slow accretion of lichens, Yusef Komunyakaa's holds the primordial slime mold.

As these poems speak of many forms of fungi, the fungi in turn serve to speak of diverse aspects of our human life: of release, mystery, and transcendence; of the hidden coinhabitances everywhere around us; of searching, fruiting, and finding. The political, social, and moral realms are also acknowledged. R.T. Smith traces an Irish reluctance to eat mushrooms back to the time of cholera and famine, and to the corpses of that period's uncountable dead. D.H. Lawrence compares the pretentious bourgeois male to a mushroom: seemingly upright, actually parasitic and riddled by worms. Adam Dickinson finds in the mushroom a complex model for "The Good," while Robert Wrigley offers an investigation of "morelity." Kay Ryan speaks of the meeting of weakness and doubt by speaking of mushrooms and symbiosis, while Pattiann Rogers and Dorianne Laux redeem the magnetisms of earthly stench.

Reading through these poems, I found myself pondering as well certain similarities between our relationships with mushrooms, poems, and poetry itself. Poems, like mushrooms, demand our close attention before they can be found or seen at all. As mushrooms are a hybrid kingdom—first thought to be plants, now believed closer to animals, but truly neither, a life form in fact uniquely their own—so it is with poems, which reside hybrid between music and speech, between logic and feeling, between waking thought and the leapings of dream, doing work they alone can. And then, as the largest living creature on earth (described in Laura Kasischke's poem) is a fungal mat whose expressed DNA extends over many square miles in Oregon's eastern forests, so poetry's mostly unseen devices underlie, sustain, and connect over vast distances other dimensions of language, whether lullaby, sermon, or political address at both its best and its worst. As mushrooms hold dangerous powers, so do poems—Plato famously banned poets from his ideal Republic because their words can sway in ways beyond reason's reach. Both mushrooms and poems hold shamanic potential; when taken inside us fully, they have the power to alter consciousness in profoundly unpredictable ways.

Neither porcini nor poems are day to day staples: continuous availability is confined to the more easily grown, more easily storable grains. Yet the intensities of the rare, the seasonal, the brief, the strange, and that which requires both a kneeling intimacy and depth of knowledge to be safely known at all—these are needed as much as oatmeal, rice, or bread. It is that elusive, concentrated presence, the sudden coming and going of life forms mostly hidden, the awareness of mysteries that can only be given, not forced into being, that both the mushrooms and the poems in this volume point toward. Gathered from the root-zones of many different trees, knife-scraped from rock-face, lifted from dung, spore-flung into air, these gathered mushroom poems offer undomestic, distinctive discoveries to all who choose to join the effort to find them.

—*Jane Hirshfield*

# INTRODUCTION

I magine something that slowly devours rocks, floats upon air and produces a trillion offspring from one fruiting body. An entity that provides a chemical phone line for trees to communicate, is the primary recycler of the planet, and makes up ten percent of the biomass of the forest. This creature has a tribe of a million and a half species, sports the largest life-forms on earth, is the alchemist of beer and wine and offers a vast array of nutritional, medicinal, industrial and mind altering substances to the animalia. A life form that lives like a plant but forms cells like an animal. We're talking about fungi.

Before plants made their way onto land, fungi arrived and paved the way for life as we know it. Today, of the estimated 150,000 mushroom species visible to the plain eye, about ten percent are known by the scientific community, and most only make a rare appearance when climate, calendar and spirit coincide. They spend their days filimentizing the soil, shaking hands with roots and traveling unseen through the atmosphere in single celled spores.

In a world obsessed with sterility, false appearances and a religious avoidance of death, decomposers can be seen as villainous, though in truth, all life depends on them. They recycle an immense amount of debris which would otherwise drown us. From their symbiotic relationship with ninety percent of plant life, mushrooms allow their sun-worshipping partners to more easily access water and nutrients from the soil. Their fruiting bodies often arrive quickly and fall back into the earth with a speed that reminds us of the fleeting nature of existence and the illusion of acquisition. They have a language all their own. Many people speak of psychedelic mushrooms revealing instructive messages to the petitioner. Those who study and hunt mushrooms learn to pick up inexplicable cues—silently spoken—as to their whereabouts.

This anthology is about fungi *speaking* through poetry. Within these pages you'll find the cream of today's poets from the powerhouse to the newly electric. Not all the poems chosen are precise;

some are just fun or witty or contextual. What might be lost in mycological thoroughness is gained in artistic sensibility, magic and accessibility.

The most dramatic elements of our world are often the hardest to replicate in art without devaluing them. In this collection we hope to impart a potent and vivid imprint of fungi as experienced by humans. We sought poems that help us find ourselves within the visions of others, strive to solve life's mysteries and provide a salve for our hearts. Twelve hundred poems later, this is what we've selected. We invite you to listen to this fungal discourse through the words of our finest poets.

—*Renée Roehl & Kelly Chadwick*

VEIL

mushroom gathering;
only the crescent moon
left unplucked

—*Sanrei*


before my hand
stretched out for the mushroom,
a butterfly breathing

—*Kobayashi Issa*


matsutake;
from the depths of the pine forest
the voice of the hawk

—*Koya*

# LOOKING FOR MUSHROOMS AT SUNRISE

*for Jean and Bill Arrowsmith*

When it is not yet day
I am walking on centuries of dead chestnut leaves
In a place without grief
Though the oriole
Out of another life warns me
That I am awake

In the dark while the rain fell
The gold chanterelles pushed through a sleep that was not mine
Waking me
So that I came up the mountain to find them

Where they appear it seems I have been before
I recognize their haunts as though remembering
Another life

Where else am I walking even now
Looking for me

*Maxine Kumin*

# THE DREAMER, THE DREAM

After the sleeper has burst his night pod
climbed up out of its silky holdings
the dream must stumble alone now
must mope in the hard eye of morning

in search of some phantom outcome
while on both sides of the tissue
the dreamer walks into the weather
past time in September woods in the rain

where the butternuts settle around him
louder than tears and in fact he comes
upon great clusters of honey mushrooms
breaking the heart of old oak

a hundred caps grotesquely piggyback
on one another, a caramel mountain
all powdered with their white spores
printing themselves in no notebook

and all this they do in secret
climbing behind his back
lumbering from their dark fissure
going up like a dream going on.

*Nance Van Winckel*

# A MUSHROOM EMERGES

in the night. Pretext
for the forest's permit
to enter the dream.

A taste left over
from the last
Crusade—shrinking

what little reason
remains
to rise.

*Sylvia Plath*

## MUSHROOMS

Overnight, very
Whitely, discreetly,
Very quietly

Our toes, our noses
Take hold on the loam,
Acquire the air.

Nobody sees us,
Stops us, betrays us;
The small grains make room.

Soft fists insist on
Heaving the needles,
The leafy bedding,

Even the paving.
Our hammers, our rams,
Earless and eyeless,

Perfectly voiceless,
Widen the crannies,
Shoulder through holes. We

Diet on water,
On crumbs of shadow,
Bland-mannered, asking

Little or nothing.
So many of us!
So many of us!

We are shelves, we are
Tables, we are meek,
We are edible,

Nudgers and shovers
In spite of ourselves.
Our kind multiplies:

We shall by morning
Inherit the earth.
Our foot's in the door.

*Yusef Komunyakaa*

## SLIME MOLDS

They're here. Among blades
Of grass, like divided cells.
Between plant & animal. Good
For nothing. In a rain storm, spores

Glom together. Yellow-white
Pieces of a puzzle. Unable to be
Seen till united. Something
Left over from a world before—

Beyond modern reason. Primeval
Fingers reduced & multiplied
A hundredfold, the most basic
Love & need shape them into a belief

System. The color of scrambled eggs.
Good for something we never thought
About, these pets of aliens crawl up
The Judas trees in bloom.

*Adam Dickinson*

# CONTRIBUTIONS TO GEOMETRY: LICHEN

Because there is no such thing as a single beginning.
Before crowberry and fireweed, among ruined boulders
that the ice let go, this slow committee.
Even now in the city, on the bark of big-boned ash,
small coastlines of lichen
are the end of the Wisconsin,
fresh melt water pooling, fingerprints plotting
new hands.
Here, in the bullish confidence of bark,
evidence that even trees
wear the beginnings of later trees.

Think of yourself as an agreement:
arms and legs in step,
each cell holding up the walls of another.
Your language is a minority government
where backbenchers rise suddenly,
threaten to cross the floor,
and what comes from your mouth
is a difficult vote.
There are two sides to every story.
North that must think south. Somewhere
in your gut other lives
remind you
with fever, stiff joints, with dream.

*Laura Kasischke*

# THE WORLD'S LARGEST LIVING THING

> *The world's largest living thing is a 2200-acre fungus*
> *in Oregon's Malheur National Forest.*

We have waited all our lives
to taste it, waited

through hate & rain, licking
the wind, spooning through the fog, while it

spread in all directions, rolled

through the forests, across the fertilized lawns. Call

it mildew, mushroom, smut. What

is it if not
the world's moldy heart?

Blood-surge, sweet meat, sleep. It is

a gorgeous sprawling brain, dreaming

you & me.

*Allan Peterson*

# UNDER AUDIOLOGY

Today we talked about my inner ear
my tympanum my cochlea
I asked about my Organs of Corti
and she knew what I couldn't
how they looked
the hidden interiors I could not see
She said did I hear "popcorn"
"mushroom" "hyphen"
I answered "polypore" "mycelia"
I was failing like dissolving deadwood
I said I heard "hyphae"
like the fungus that undergirds Michigan
that there seemed to be a veil
separating me from emergent meaning
She mentioned the labyrinth
and fluid build up that scrambles frequencies
But the words were like nutrients
Instead of mishearing I was listening
to something pushing urgently into the light

*Ted Kooser*

## THE MUSHROOM HUNTERS

In the green cathedral of nettles,
in the incense of dew, in the hymn
of mosquitoes, under the high
black-raftered, yawning vault of oaks
where a dove takes on the shape
of praying hands and wood ticks
sit in their pews of rotted logs
and wait for the cup to come round,
we guiltless, tiptoe thieves,
in single file with empty paper bags,
approach the lacy, plum-blossom
altar of Spring, upon which
a few fat yellow candles stand
as if they'd been placed there to wait
for the flames of our hands.

*David Axelrod*

# GEORGIC: FOR MY FRIENDS
# WHO NEVER FIND ANY

Like the universe, that's how wild
mushrooms grow from forest mold:

everywhere is the center, find one
pitted cone and spiral outward

in concentric rings. By this method
you'll pick all you need to fill a basket

with black morels, any morning in May,
when heart-leaf arnica covers forest floor

in unbroken green that ripples like a pond
whenever wind tires of the pinetops

and comes down to search among
the modest things closer to ground.

You'll need to squat down a great deal,
pray to the mountain's god, who answers,

booming overhead or pelting you with
sleet and hail. You'll need to get close,

peer under the green shadow of arnica—
canopy nearest earth, someone else's

heaven, the sky of a world that's always
underfoot, trampled, ignored, very much

like the other world you know better.
But here, you visit only during a few weeks

each spring, your giant face reappearing
like a rare planet in its eccentric orbit.

That means you spiral, too, your life
another ring in a pattern of rings

with a random center of gravity.
Or there's no gravity

and you're one among many wanderers
wobbling blind through space, until

that metaphor evaporates like sleet and hail
melting back into sun-lit air, and you're just

standing here at the edge of a dark grove
of Douglas fir that didn't fall to a chainsaw,

and right here at the margin between
what was destroyed and what wasn't,

you clap your hands, laugh, and quickly kneel.

*Robert Penn Warren*

# HAVE YOU EVER EATEN STARS?

*A Note on Mycology*

Scene:    A glade on a bench of the mountain,
Where beech, birch, and spruce meet
In peace, though in peace not intermingled,
Around the slight hollow, upholstered
In woods-earth damp, and soft, centuries old—
Spruce needle, beech leaf, birch leaf, ground-pine belly-crawling,
And fern frond, and deadfall of birch, grass blade
So biblically frail, and sparse in that precinct where
The sunray makes only its brief
And perfunctory noontide visitation.
All, all in that cycle's beneficence
Of being are slowly absorbed—oh, slowly—into
What once had fed them. And now,
In silence as absolute as death,
Or as vision in breathlessness,
Your foot may come. Or mine,
As when I, sweat-soaked in summer's savagery,
Might here come, and stand
In that damp cool, and peace of process,
And here, somewhere, a summer-thinned brook descending,
Past stone, and stone its musical stair.

But late, once in the season's lateness, I,
After drouth had broken, rain come and gone,
And sky been washed to a blue more delicate,
Came. Stood. Stared. For now,
Earth, black as a midnight sky,
Was, like sky-darkness, studded with
Gold stars, as though

In emulation, however brief.
There, by a deer trail, by deer dung nourished,
Burst the gleam, rain-summoned,
Of bright golden chanterelles.
However briefly, however small and restricted, here was
A glade-burst of glory.

Later, I gathered stars into a basket.


Question:     What can you do with stars, or glory?
I'll tell you, I'll tell you—thereof
Eat. Swallow. Absorb. Let bone
Be sustained thereof, let gristle
Toughen, flesh be more preciously
Gratified, muscle yearn in
Its strength. Let brain glow
In its own midnight of darkness,
Under its own inverted, bowl-shaped
Sky, skull-sky, let the heart
Rejoice.
          What other need now
Is possible to you but that
Of seeing life as glory?

*Adam Dickinson*

# THE GOOD

The good itself could be a mushroom,
may wear a crown after all,
require a certain humidity: logs,
tree stumps, bathroom tiles,
those cumulus brains
in the late afternoon
over hot prairie towns.

No one can explain the sickles
of dead grass in the yard
when mushrooms leave.
A revolution without hammers.
No one can say what goes wrong
when, half-hearted, attention divided,
we can't bring ourselves to finish
our holy designs.

The greatest moral works
are mushrooms.
They reveal themselves as this.
Take the Bible, take
the Geneva Convention.
Look at the curves of dead ground.
Take the Communist Manifesto;
it needs very little light.

For some time, we expected
the end of the world
to be a mushroom.
A vengeful good, a good

of fire, clouded thought.
But every spring they come out of the ground
like universal suffrage,
a writ of *habeas corpus*,
speech before writing.
They say, dirt. They say, get up.

*Jane Whitledge*

## MOREL MUSHROOMS

Softly they come
thumbing up from
firm ground

protruding unharmed.
Easily crumbled
and yet

how they shouldered
the leaf and mold
aside, rising

unperturbed,
breathing obscurely,
still as stone.

By the slumping log,
by a dappled aspen,
they grow alone.

A dumb eloquence
seems their trade.
Like hooded monks

in a sacred wood
they say:
Tomorrow we are gone.

*Gerald Stern*

# THE SWEETNESS OF LIFE

After the heavy rain we were able to tell about the mushrooms,
which ones made us sick, which ones had the dry bitterness,
which ones caused stomach pains and dizziness and hallucinations.

It was the beginning of religion again—on the river—
all the battles and ecstasies and persecutions
taking place beside the hackberries and the fallen locust.

I sat there like a lunatic,
weeping, raving standing on my head, living
in three and four and five places at once.

I sat there letting the wild and the domestic combine,
finally accepting the sweetness of life,
on my own mushy log,
in the white and spotted moonlight.

*William Stafford*

# BRING THE NORTH

Mushroom, Soft Ear, Old Memory,
Root Come to Tell the Air:
bring the Forest Floor along
the valley; bring all that comes
blue into passes, long shores
around a lake, talk, talk, talk
miles, then deep. Bring that story.

Unfold a pack by someone's door—
wrapped in leather, brought in brown,
what the miles collect.
Leave sound in an empty
house in its own room there,
a little cube hung like a birdcage
in the attic, with a swinging door.
Search out a den: try natural,
no one's, your own, a dirt
floor. Accept them all.

One way to find your place is like
the rain, a million requests
for lodging, one that wins, finds
your cheek: you find your home,
a storm that walks the waves.
You hear that cloak whip, those
chilly hands take night apart.
In split Heaven you see one sudden
eye on yours, and yours in it,
scared, falling, fallen.

Mushroom, Soft Ear, Memory,
attend what is.
Bring the North.

David Mason

# IN THE MUSHROOM SUMMER

Colorado turns Kyoto in a shower,
mist in the pines so thick the crows delight
(or seem to), winging in obscurity.
The ineffectual panic of a squirrel
who chattered at my passing gave me pause
to watch his Ponderosa come and go—
long needles scratching cloud. I'd summited
but knew it only by the wildflower meadow,
the muted harebells, paintbrush, gentian,
scattered among the locoweed and sage.
Today my grief abated like water soaking
underground, its scar a little path
of twigs and needles winding ahead of me
downhill to the next bend. Today I let
the rain soak through my shirt and was unharmed.

*Lynne Shapiro*

## MUSHROOMS AND MODERN LIVING

More than mountains and rivers,
interior design affects us.

Seek positive energy:
whenever possible apply mushroom-colored paint
to walls and furniture.

The feng shui expert examines office metabolism
for potential germination of disharmony,
places mirrors carefully to allow spores full circulation.

When approaching unstoppable mushrooms in the woods,
I maintain a position of stability and peace, enhance my chi,
and give them the right of way.

# MUSHROOM RIVER

Crazy Horse picked one the size of his fist.
Underneath, gills, as in the heads of fish.
He knew it could hear him. He said,
I am going to eat you, & did.

& later, sleeping, saw himself walking
where friends he had not seen since childhood
welcomed him. To be heard, they did not need
to open their mouths. Their campfire

was a river flowing round on itself,
filled with huge silver buffalo
with red eyes. There was nothing to do here
but stare into the current, & forget, & remember.

*Gary Snyder*

## THE WILD MUSHROOM

Well the sunset rays are shining
Me and Kai have got our tools
A basket and a trowel
And a book with all the rules

Don't ever eat Boletus
If the tube-mouths they are red
Stay away from the Amanitas
Or brother you are dead

Sometimes they're already rotten
Or the stalks are broken off
Where the deer have knocked them over
While turning up the duff

We set out in the forest
To seek the wild mushroom
In shapes diverse and colorful
Shining through the woodland gloom

If you look out under oak trees
Or around an old pine stump
You'll know a mushroom's coming
By the way the leaves are humped

They send out multiple fibers
Through the roots and sod
Some make you mighty sick they say
Or bring you close to God

So here's to the mushroom family
A far-flung friendly clan
For food, for fun, for poison
They are a help to man.

*Christopher Howell*

## LETTING THINGS GO

So now I'm thinking about mushrooms,
their curious smell and lightness,
about the great adventure of not knowing
exactly which were poison
and which would get you off like Flash Gordon
in a purple car, about how we wandered pastures
plucking and praying for the wild ride
that seldom came.

And in that connection I have to think
of 1974, Montana Bill and I driving all the way
to Manzanillo in a Dodge van
to present my manuscript of poems to
John Muir Publications
at their annual conference and drug fest.
After days of negotiations, it was agreed
I would read to the twenty or more principal mavens
of the group, including Muir himself, and they
would decide.

We gathered around a huge table out
under the stars
and I opened my manuscript . . .
but *first*, Muir said, we should "get into the mood"
and began to load his pipe with a weed
and *psilocybe mexicana* mixture which everyone
smoked until their eyes were huge, pulsing zeros.

Then I read. It was like hollering
into a vat of butter, like singing to Martians
about the stock exchange.

When, after three hundred years, I finished,
they nodded into themselves, looked around
and went off toward the beach.
Two days later the managing editor collared me
and said, "Well, they thought I should talk to you
because we're about the same height. So,
it's like this, we know you're a good poet
and we'd really like to help you out, but
you're into holding onto things

and we're into letting things go."

*Alberto Ríos*

## PRAYERS TO THE DANGEROUS

Pretty girls go walking away to prayers.
What they pray for, C-shaped, is not so different:
Homemade waffles, omelettes black with mushrooms,
Mouthfuls of mushrooms—
One girl thinks of fire: in his hands, his eyelids
As they drooped, that halfway excruciation
Coming from a moment without a name yet,
Pressing, and biting.

Boy. You never told me about the burning
Fires you'd leave inside, how an inside's burning
Makes a blackness there, where the black is empty,
Charred like a night's sky,
Sky the sun has burnt and then left, with embers
There instead of stars, like the Elks club picnic
Finished, charcoal stars as the only warm things
Drunk men can talk to.
Danger boy, you could have remembered my skin.
I remember you, how I swallowed tender
Words you had inside, on your tongue, all water.
Hands, that they touched me.

C-shaped on her pew, in that lean of children praying,
One girl only dreams of the ripest mushrooms,
Undersides of mushrooms, that color, pepper.
These are her prayers:
How, as food, she wishes for him, his touching.
That his fire leaves a black in her mouth, her eyes, her
Fisted hands, means a place for his returning.
These are her prayers.

*Xue Di*

# THE MUSHROOM RIVER

That river is filled with mushrooms
  Yes, mother. The river you soaked your hands in
  My past flows by. The child in his red jacket exposes the
  skin of daylight. He is picking mushrooms on the river, his
  basket full of smiles
  Do not enter the dark misery of the forest. Mother

come back to the fairy tales with me:
  grandma hides the wolf in your voice, baring the day's teeth
  It's getting dark again. Will my love get lost? Mother, my
  childhood is gone forever
  Your hands bring the sound of water brimming from my eyes
  Do not go the lonely path of old age. Mother

Mushrooms. Butterflies dance in your silver hair
  The light is on. I walk towards you, along the river. The
  wolf in the fairy tale will die too, and the child do riffs
  on its teeth to go with the beautiful sounds of the road
  Memory pushes up like no end of pale, floating mushrooms
  carrying off the last of your years
  Go back inside. Don't stand in pain, waiting for me
  Remember how my poems send signals. I'll bring you songs of
  the vast fields

I'll describe for you the mushroom river

*Tomaz Salamun*

## LITTLE MUSHROOMS

So this is how the whole thing goes
by far the best are the little mushrooms
little mushrooms in the soup
nada nada nada nada
                    fiuuuuu one little mushroom
this little green parsley in tuxedo
and darkness for a long time
then they run to get a cleaning lady
responsible for all of this
nothing nothing nothing nothing
                    fiuuuuuuu one more little mushroom
healthy though
the blood is not so great
because she got hepatitis
Heavy heavy are these little mushrooms
heavy in the Holy Mother

*Donna J. Gelagotis Lee*

# ODE TO FUNGI-FILLED FACE CREAM

Sweet fungi-filled face cream,
    release your promises.

Quell the skin's inflammation and prod
    each cell to turn over as I turn in my sleep.

Bring your earthy toughness to ravaged ravines.
    Tone of tough fiber. Hypsizygus ulmarius and

Chaga, protect me from my harsh environment.
    Extract of Elm Oyster that sprouts from wounds

on the tree, keep me from being inflamed:
    ulm/elm, veil-less, edible, solitary mushroom

found high on box elders, attach your essence
    to me. O Chaga, *Inonotus obliquus,*

potent mushroom of immortality, help me face
    the world with calm. Heal me.

*John Bargowski*

## 7 PRECIOUS MUSHROOMS

      I offer up the morning ache,
lean against the mulberry
seeking intercession under the yellowing leaves
while keeping an eye on the crows
in the garden with their dagger bills
and hoarse croaks,
      and the phoebe,
who will not leave her garden post
until the ground crusts over
and the mud-colored doves begin to gather
in little groups of five or six.
      I will whisper this tonight
before bed, after my wife has dabbed her hops
and lavender behind each ankle,
spread oil of frankincense across
her sutured chest
      and begun to count the thirty drops
of the *7 Precious Mushrooms,*
      and I will sign myself
the way the old priests taught,
chant praise to the flower-like shiitake,
the Red Reishi and Lion's Mane,
      praise the common
coriolus, the Ram's Head, the holy
cordyceps and veiled agaricus,
all potent builders of macrophage
and t-cell function,
      praise the phoebe on her ritual post
and the dove descending from the power lines
to disappear between the hoed furrows,

bless even the crow—wild-eyed
and belligerent—
        as I watch my beloved dip her finger
into the potion, the water glass cloud,
then clear to the brim,
under her stir.

*Arthur Sze*

# EARTHSTAR

Opening the screen door, you find a fat spider
poised at the threshold. When I swat it,

hundreds of tiny crawling spiders burst out.
What space in the mind bursts into waves

of wriggling light? As we round a bend,
a gibbous moon burnishes lava rocks and waves.

A wild boar steps into the road, and, around
another bend, a mongoose darts across our headlights.

As spokes to a hub, the very far converges
to the very near. A row of Siberian irises

buds and blooms in the yard behind our bedroom.
A moth flutters against a screen and sets

off a light. I had no idea carded wool spun
into yarn could be dipped and oxidized into bliss.

Once, hunting for chanterelles in a meadow,
I flushed quail out of the brush. Now

you step on an unexpected earthstar, and it
bursts in a cloud of brown spores into June light.

*Emily Dickinson*

## THE ELF OF PLANTS

The Mushroom is the Elf of Plants—
At Evening, it is not—
At Morning, in a Truffled Hut
It stop upon a Spot

As if it tarried always
And yet its whole Career
Is shorter than a Snake's Delay
And fleeter than a Tare—

'Tis Vegetation's Juggler—
The Germ of Alibi—
Doth like a Bubble antedate
And like a Bubble, hie—

I feel as if the Grass was pleased
To have it intermit—
This surreptitious scion
Of Summer's circumspect.

Had Nature any supple Face
Or could she one contemn—
Had Nature an Apostate—
That Mushroom—it is Him!

*Elizabeth Bishop*

## THE SHAMPOO

The still explosions on the rocks,
the lichens, grow
by spreading, gray, concentric shocks.
They have arranged
to meet the rings around the moon, although
within our memories they have not changed.

And since the heavens will attend
as long on us,
you've been, dear friend,
precipitate and pragmatical;
and look what happens. For Time is
nothing if not amenable.

The shooting stars in your black hair
in bright formation
are flocking where,
so straight, so soon?
—Come, let me wash it in this big tin basin,
battered and shiny like the moon.

*A.R. Ammons*

# THE GRASS MIRACLES

The grass miracles have kept me down all autumn
purpose turning on me like an inward division
The grasses heading barbed tufts
airy panicles and purple spikes
have kept me stalled in the deadends
of branching dreams
        It is as though I had started up the trunk
and then dispersed like ant trails
along the branches
and out on the twigs
and paused dipping with a golden thought
at the points of the leaves

A black stump hidden
in grass and old melon vines
has reined my hurry
and I have gone up separately
        jiggling like a bubble flock
in globes of time

I have not been industrious this autumn
It has seemed necessary
to accomplish everything with a pause
        bending to part the grass
to what round fruit
becoming entangled in clusters
tying all the future up
in variations on present miracles

*W.S. Merwin*

## FIELD MUSHROOMS

I never gave a thought to them at first
with their white heads
cut into slices
under a water of plastic on a blue
section of carpet
or even hanging in a scale
like the piled ruins of a foot

I was shown that when the right time came
you could overturn a dry cowpat
by the edge of a long green swamp
late on a cold
Autumn afternoon
as the sun was going down
and there underneath
the real white heads were still growing

I went on finding them
always at evening
coming to recognize a depth
in the shade of oaks and chestnuts
a quickening in the moss year after year
a suggestion of burning
signs of something already there in it's own place
a texture of flesh
scarcely born
full of the knowledge of darkness

# FRUITING BODY

nightly coming
mushroom thieves
clappers set

—*Teijiro*


ribbed white canopy
an overnight sensation
hell-bent for salad

—*David Alan Foster*


cook's worn-out shoes
slow and careful among
the new mushrooms

—*Ferris Gilli*

*W. B. Yeats*

# A DAWN-SONG

From the waves the sun hath reeled,
  Proudly in his saffron walking;
Sleep in some far other field
  Goes his poppies now a-hawking;
From the hills of earth have pealed
  Murmurs of her children talking—
My companions, two and two,
Gathering mushrooms in the dew.

Wake, *ma cushla,* sleepy-headed;
  Trembles as a bell of glass
All heaven's floor, with vapours bedded—
  And along the mountains pass,
With their mushrooms lightly threaded
  On their swaying blades of grass,
Lads and lasses, two and two,
Gathering mushrooms in the dew.

Wake! the heron, rising, hath
  Showered away the keen dew drops;
Weasel warms him on the path,
  Half asleep the old cow crops,
In the fairy-haunted rath,
  Dewy-tongued, the daisy tops—
We will wander, I and you,
Gathering mushrooms in the dew.

For your feet the morning prayeth:
  We will find her favourite lair,
Straying as the heron strayeth,

As the moorfowl and the hare,
While the morning star decayeth
   In the bosom of the air—
Gayest wanderers, I and you,
Gathering mushrooms in the dew.

*Michael J. Rosen*

## A SPRING OF MORELS

bright dappling puzzles
the forest floor, already
in pieces since fall

.

spring's first warm nights
sweeping branch, my second hand,
loses track of time

.

worn trails through wild woods
then a new path's loose, dark soil
what else can love clear?

.

amid canopies
of may apple, our steps are
the understory

.

the year's first morel!
now pupils can recall not
where to look but how

.

thick strips of elm bark
ring a bare trunk: blond morels
half-bent as we are

.

old brittle basket
searching for mushrooms again
to carry us back

.

are they here . . . or here?
we hunt with memory's frost
as the morning warms

.

side by side since dawn . . .
here's one . . . found one . . . suddenly
we find we're shouting

.

conceding untold
mushrooms, we leave . . . they raise up
like hands with answers

.

these loud, crisp, browned leaves—
last June's shade, fall's reds—will soon
be hope's rich humus

*Robert Wrigley*

## MORELITY

Heavy thatch of leaf and needle,
    sun-mottled also,
so the eye you need to find them
    almost always fails.

But when you do, their dark knuckles
    rucking up the duff,
their airy reticular brains
    bobbing in the air

and breathing a sexual musk—
    after that they're everywhere.
Your grocery bag grows as heavy
    as a child, and limp,

as if plucked up they could only sleep
    and dream, of how the sun
they had yearned for awaits them
    in the butter's slick

and a skillet's sublunary
    bed, where they'll sizzle
from fungal unto meat
    which you will take and eat.

David Young

# HUNTING FOR MUSHROOMS
# IN ORANGE COUNTY

Like a snail on a cabbage leaf
I move along this hillside.

Blank eyeballs bulging in the grass,
doorknobs to darkness, night's white knuckles,
the scattered cups and saucers of the dead,
old smoky hard-ons coaxed up by the rain!

There are stars and flowers in this world,
green sprouts, plump nuts, threshed grain,
fruit in bright rinds and clusters—

but there are these buttons too,
these pallid lamps, lit by a secret,
tokens so strange we hold our breath to eat them,
puffball, campestris, morel,
wrinkled and chalky blebs of foam.

I look up from my gathering
and think I don't know where I am,
the buckskin hills, the instant cities,
this grainy earth we find and lose
and find again
and learn to say we shall lie down in,

meanwhile nibbling on these swollen caps
beautiful messages of decay, from roots, bones, teeth,
from coal and bark, humus and pulp and sperm,
muzzle-skull, channel and hand, the all-containing
   dead,

invisible branchings of our living smolder—
I glance around me, half-bewildered,
here in this California sunlight
spore dust drifting right through my body

a meadow-mushroom humming between my fingers.

*Nance Van Winckel*

# FRIENDS IN THEIR HELICOPTER CIRCLING

Not far from the given place
and close enough to the given time,
I was out gathering the ripe morels
in dense woods. Startled from my servitude
by the rains.—And by the whirl overhead.
My friends' gaze stayed hidden
in the pines' ever widening skirts,
though our affection for their airs
trembled in a rotorized mist.

My bag was loaded deep with spores
of barely digested pasts. And by my feet
the mistake I'd picked up last: Mr. slimy
slug, and where in the world were his eyes?
I saw his slime feelers extend
and retract. They navigated an idea
of earth. But no clue about
the sky. As my friends zinged it,
the air, a quick goodbye meant for me.

They were off to count the gone and
going elk. Farewell. Off to cold pastures
farther north, where among census takers
those first pure solitudes began.
And bye to the big blades blowing past,
I stepped into the clearing. So long,
we waved upwards and downwards—until
at the designated spot between many moving
hands, our waves were met upon the air.

*Louis Jenkins*

## MUSHROOM HUNTING

Here I am, as usual, wandering vaguely through a dark wood. Just
when I think I know something, when I think I have discerned some
pattern, a certain strategy—ah, they grow on the north edge of the
low mossy spots—I find one on top of a rise and it shoots my theory
all to hell. Every time I find one it's a surprise. The truth is there
is no thought that goes into this. These things just pop up. And all
this thinking, this human consciousness, isn't what it's cracked up to
be. Some inert matter somehow gets itself together, pokes itself up
from the ground, gets some ideas and goes walking around, wanting
and worrying, gets angry, takes a kick at the dog and falls apart.

*John Cage*

## *from* SILENCE   *(p. 264)*

There's a street in Stony Point in a lowland near the river where a
number of species of mushrooms grow abundantly. I visit this street
often. A few years ago in May I found the morel there, a choice
mushroom which is rare around Rockland County. I was delighted.
None of the people living on this street ever talk to me while I'm
collecting mushrooms. Sometimes children come over and kick at
them before I get to them. Well, the year after I found the morel,
I went back in May expecting to find it again, only to discover that
a cinder-block house had been put up where the mushroom had
been growing. As I looked at the changed land, all the people in the
neighborhood came out on their porches. One of them said, "Ha,
ha! Your mushrooms are gone."

## *from* A YEAR FROM MONDAY   *(p. 69)*

After an hour or so in the woods looking for mushrooms, Dad said,
"Well, we can always go and buy some real ones."

When Vera Williams first noticed that I was interested in wild mushrooms, she told her children not to touch any of the them because they were all deadly poisonous. A few days later she bought a steak at Martino's and decided to serve it smothered with mushrooms. When she started to cook the mushrooms, the children all stopped whatever they were doing and watched her attentively. When she served dinner, they all burst into tears.

*D.H. Lawrence*

## HOW BEASTLY THE BOURGEOIS IS

How beastly the bourgeois is
especially the male of the species—

Presentable, eminently presentable—
shall I make you a present of him?

Isn't he handsome? Isn't he healthy? Isn't he a fine specimen?
Doesn't he look the fresh clean Englishman, outside?
Isn't it God's own image? tramping his thirty miles a day
after partridges, or a little rubber ball?
wouldn't you like to be like that, well off, and quite the thing?

Oh, but wait!
Let him meet a new emotion, let him be faced with another man's need,
let him come home to a bit of moral difficulty, let life face him
    with a new demand on his understanding
and then watch him go soggy, like a wet meringue.
Watch him turn into a mess, either a fool or a bully.
Just watch the display of him, confronted with a new demand on his
    intelligence,
a new life-demand.

How beastly the bourgeois is
especially the male of the species—

Nicely groomed, like a mushroom
standing there so sleek and erect and eyeable—
and like a fungus, living on the remains of bygone life
sucking his life out of the dead leaves of greater life than his own.

And even so, he's stale, he's been there too long.
Touch him, and you'll find he's all gone inside
just like an old mushroom, all wormy inside, and hollow
under a smooth skin and an upright appearance.

Full of seething, wormy, hollow feelings
rather nasty—
How beastly the bourgeois is!

Standing in their thousands, these appearances, in damp England
what a pity they can't all be kicked over
like sickening toadstools, and left to melt back, swiftly
into the soil of England.

*Richard Wilbur*

## CHILDREN OF DARKNESS

If groves are choirs and sanctuaried fanes,
What have we here?
An elm-bole cocks a bloody ear;
In the oak's shadow lies a strew of brains.
Wherever, after the deep rains,

The woodlands are morose and reek of punk,
The gobbets grow—
Tongue, lobe, hand, hoof or butchered toe
Amassing on the fallen branch half-sunk
In leaf-mold, or the riddled trunk.

Such violence done, it comes as no surprise
To notice next
How some, parodically sexed,
Puff, blush, or gape, while shameless phalloi rise,
To whose slimed heads come carrion flies.

Their gift is not for life, these creatures who
Disdain to root,
Will bear no stem or leaf, no fruit,
And, mimicking the forms which they eschew,
Make it their pleasure to undo

All that has heart and fiber. Yet of course
What these break down
Wells up refreshed in branch and crown.
May we not after all forget that Norse
Drivel of Wotan's panicked horse,

And every rumor bred of forest-fear?
Are these the brood
Of adders? Are they devil's food,
Minced witches, or the seed of rutting deer?
Nowhere does water stand so clear

As in stalked cups where pine has come to grief;
The chanterelle
And cèpe are not the fare of hell;
Where coral schools the beech and aspen leaf
To seethe like fishes of a reef,

Light strikes into a gloom in which are found
Red disc, grey mist,
Gold-auburn firfoot, amethyst,
Food for the eye whose pleasant stinks abound,
And dead men's fingers break the ground.

Gargoyles is what they are at worst, and should
They preen themselves
On being demons, ghouls, or elves,
The holy chiaroscuro of the wood
Still would embrace them. They are good.

*Sidney Wade*

## PLUTEUS PETASATUS

Night. A mute white dwarf
in earthmoving hat
bulbs up from the mold.

It has nudged and shoved
its smart headstrong head
through the discrete wood.

Now its exquisite
fruiting body feeds
on the broke-down else,

infiltrates the blank
detritus of lives,
and rises and smells

like a star. This is
degenerate news,
the small moonlit kind.

*Arthur Sze*

# MUSHROOM HUNTING
# IN THE JEMEZ MOUNTAINS

Walking in a mountain meadow toward the north slope,
I see redcap amanitas with white warts and know
they signal cepes. I see a few colonies of puffballs,
red russulas with chalk-white stipes, brown-gilled
Poison Pie. In the shade under spruce are two
red-pored boletes: slice them in half and the flesh
turns blue in seconds. Under fir is a single amanita
with basal cup, flaring annulus, white cap: is it
the Rocky Mountain form of *Amanita pantherina?*
I am aware of danger in naming, in misidentification,
in imposing the distinctions of a taxonomic language
onto the things themselves. I know I have only
a few hours to hunt mushrooms before early afternoon rain.
I know it is a mistake to think I am moving and
that agarics are still: they are more transient
than we acknowledge, more susceptible to full moon,
to a single rain, to night air, to a moment of sunshine.
I know in this meadow my passions are mycorrhizal
with nature. I may shout out ecstasies, aches, griefs,
and hear them vanish in the white-pored silence.

*Lee Upton*

## SOME OF THE MEMBERS
## OF MY FAMILY ARE POISONOUS

*Amanita vírosa,*
whiter than Moby Dick, whiter
than aspirin, "Destroying
Angel," unlike
*Amanita rubescens* which
is a peeled wall
a pillar kicked over in a desert.
*Amanita pantherina*
is flesh pumped with air.
Look here. A stiff wind blew this skirt up.
This one opens like a mussel shell
astonished at steam. Here's a
thin-stemmed lily pad,
a canopy at Monaco.
These other improvisations
are meant for the ocean floor.
Coral wafted,
low to wind currents.
Here's a crumpled hat
Hades spat into.
A foot cushion of proliferating cells,
fleshy prongs,
a spirit whittled down to the nerves
seething like sap in a fire.
Here's the setting for a casino full of slots,
a compressed feather duster,
a brain jelly pickled with plots,
hallucinating suffocation. But

my favorite uncle
is the littlest devil
pounded into the earth while standing,
right up to his purple horns.

*Gary Snyder*

## WHITE STICKY

Glancing up through oaks
        dry leaves still hanging on,
        some tilt
        and airy wobble down, dry settles.
Pale early sun,
        standing in damp leaf ground
        pine needles, by dirt road,
        holding Gen's hand,
        waiting for his ride to school.

We talk about mushrooms.
This year was good
        but most got eaten by worms.
There, under manzanita, more white stickies.
Can't find the bookname—
        glowing white and gooey cap,
        an unknown
        that we call "White Sticky" which is good
        as any name.

He goes off in Mike's old car to school,
        I walk back to the house
        try once more the mushroom book.

        *(Hygrophorus?)*

*Gary Young*

# EATING WILD MUSHROOMS

After the rain, when the earth releases
a little wheezing breath and loosens
its brittle hold on the surface of things,

wild mushrooms appear under the trees,
against logs and along the rotting
boards behind the barn. I see them lift

the ground under the quince and spread
the scallions apart and rise, and open.
I have been shown by those who know

the slick-skinned Blewit, the Prince
like a man's head, and Satyr's Beard
with this yellow mange. But for the rest

I cultivate an ignorance and pick
puffballs a particular shade of beige,
toadstools with the prettiest caps

or purple, spongy stem. What I don't know
can't hurt me. What I do know
is that mushrooms rise from the dead

to die again, to enter the death
of whatever enters the earth. When I
pick an unfamiliar mushroom and eat it

the ground gives up for once and is cheated.
It is like kissing a stranger on the mouth
It is knowing what you are and being forgiven.

*Pattiann Rogers*

# GEOCENTRIC

Indecent, self-soiled, bilious
reek of turnip and toadstool
decay, dribbling the black oil
of wilted succulents, the brown
fester of rotting orchids,
in plain view, that stain
of stinkhorn down your front,
that leaking roil of bracket
fungi down your back, you
purple-haired, grainy-fuzzed
smolder of refuse, fathering
fumes and boils and powdery
mildews, enduring the constant
interruption of sink-mire
flatulence, contagious
with ear wax, corn smut,
blister rust, backwash
and graveyard debris, rich
with manure bog and dry-rot
harboring not only egg-addled
garbage and wrinkled lip
of orange-peel mold but also
the clotted breath of overripe
radish and burnt leek, bearing
every dank, malodorous rut
and scarp, all sulphur fissures
and fetid hillside seepages, old,
*old,* dependable, engendering
forever the stench and stretch
and warm seethe of inevitable
putrefaction, nobody
loves you as I do.

*Ann Lauinger*

# WILD MUSHROOMS

Never mind getting to know our names:
Slippery Jill, Green Stain, Stinky Squid,
Inky Cap, Angel's Wings, Devil's Urn.
What you need to know is anonymous.
We are earth's organs, her oracles.
Ask what you will, there's only one answer:
*self is a fraud*—flim-flam phoenix,
articulate toy, a tease to distract
for a time—no ticket to eternity.
All marvels, mechanisms, mastery—
mere matter. All suffer their metamorphoses.
What do you want with wild flowers?
Let the sun, senile and oversexed,
lavish his light on their lying designs.
Turn aside, step to the sunless
margins of the path. With moss and mold
we hold dank dominion here. On dung
and leaf-litter, living and lifeless wood,
our flesh unfolds. Here is your fellowship:
sacks and caps and cups and cortex
fringed coral fingers and fat thumbs
sponge of bone-marrow, birthmarks, blotches
bright cinnabar beads of blood.

*Gary Young*

The signature mark of autumn has arrived at last with the
rains: orange of pumpkin, orange persimmon, orange lichen
on rocks and fallen logs; a copper moon hung low over the
orchard; moist, ruddy limbs of the madrone, russet oak leaf,
storm-peeled redwood, acorns emptied by squirrels and jays;
and mushrooms, orange boletes, Witch's Butter sprouting on
rotted oak, the Deadly Galerina, and of course, chanterelles,
which we'll eat tonight with pasta, goat cheese, and wine.

*Harry Gilonis*

# BEEFSTEAK FUNGUS

*Fistulina hepatica* for David Hutchens

meaty analogies:

a piece of liver
jutting out from a trunk.


dark red, marbled.
juicy;

druids grew it,

knights guarded
the trees
it lived on

an
ox tongue

prime,

raw

*Harry Gilonis*

## OYSTER FUNGUS

*Pleurotus ostreatus* for Catherine Gilonis, for Eugene Watters

found in the
skull of a
stranded whale

reversing decay
on rotten
logs

turning multiple
rumps
to the moon

small scallops
from a
bough

casseroled
in
béchamel

*Harry Gilonis*

## FLY AGARIC

*Amanita muscaria* for Paul Holman, for Grass and for Pynchon

inside each
persimmon-coloured cap's
pellicle:

God's body.

Feed the fungus
to mares, and
drink their urine

or to your servants
and drink theirs

mixed
with bilberry juice

*Christine Boyka Kluge*

## TOADSTOOLS

Soft umbrellas
of the underworld
push up
through beaded moss,
spokes rusted with spores,
eager for wind.

## TURKEY TAIL

Its gray-green mummy ear
clings to the maple stump,
listening
for the first hoarse whisper
of rain.

*Robert Michael Pyle*

# CHINOOK AND CHANTERELLE

What gifts these are
from river and woods. These
coral ones, muscled strumpets, plucked
from the fishers' nets
where the shrunken runs
still shine. And these
golden ones, fluted trumpets, pinched
from the forest floor
where the second-growth hemlocks
still stand. Surely
we are unworthy of such as these!

But if enjoyment of succulent flesh
is any mitigation; if the tongue's
fierce possession of taste
can be extenuation; if the way
we chew and praise and slurp and swallow
and—say it—*worship* this fin and stipe,
these silver scales and meaty caps,
can sing the hard shimmer
in the stream can cry the soft glimmer
on the mossy floor can save us—
if these gestures make
any difference whatsoever, well,
then maybe we deserve them
after all.

R. *T. Smith*

## MUSHROOMS

*Sneem, County Kerry*

When I offer to sauté
a gathering in
chardonnay and butter,

my host declines, says
some bog Irish still
won't touch nocturnal

volunteers. In the time
of coffin ships,
cholera, and famine

his ancestors and mine
made do on winkles,
dog soup, and nettles.

"Might as well snare
a brace of crows
as eat the Saxon

Witches' tits." Owen
still blames English
greed, the velvet gentry,

and priests. He claims
a ghostly fungus still
thrives from the rainy

west to Dublin. "We
ate God's body and died
in the ditches. Yer

man the toadstool sprung
up from the corpses,
same color as spuds,

or cassocks. The urchins
ate them, but never
again. We'd rather starve."

And when I argue for
the medicine of forgetting
and haute cuisine—

a slew of scrumptious
buttons—he tips
his Guinness glass

steep, backhands
the lather from his
lips: "No need

for buttons on a shroud."

*Alan Dugan*

## RISING IN FALL,

the mushrooms feel like stiff pricks made of rot.
Oh spreading glans, what
a botanical striving to butt
hogberry branches and leaves apart
to rise to fuck the sky so fast,
six inches in, up IT, with dirt
on top of each umbrella ribbed beneath,
in one night after rain. Stars,
there is life down here in the dark.
It wants you, upward, but not much.
The mushrooms die so fast
in their external manifestations that
their maggots working to be flies
make moving liquid of their blackening heads.
Oh you can see them falling downward for a week
to dirt—that's when they really live—
and then the flies take off.
How high do they get to sting us?
Not high. It's ridiculous. I ask
a woman, "Do you get the point
of all this pointless action?"
She answers, "Naturally. Yes. Idiot."

## GENITAL

The texture's genital, no argument there.
Coveted brains of the morel, secreted
in spring beneath old orchard trees;

muscled portobellos, their dark-finned
juice; woody stems of shiitake;
golden-trumpet chanterelles; or

chicken of the woods, a spongy sulphur—
I have chewed them all, and thought
of men, blood's resurrection of shaft

and head, the furry grunt and thrust,
the milky jet, the sticky after-drowse,
the nights and nights of never enough.

Without wheedling for consent
I take up agaricus, porcini, puff ball,
slide their flesh and heat inside me,

common substitutes for what's rich
and rare, those black-goateed gods
I would much prefer devouring.

The age will come, I presume, when
cheesy mushroom enchiladas, crisp
strudels, scallop and mushroom pies

will prove sufficient, when plump
comfort will overbalance longing.
I await such peace with stiff impatience.

*Jim Daniels*

# SIN WITH A LITTLE GOD IN IT

*Truffle Fest, Norcia, Umbria*

We stumbled uphill, uneven over the old stones,
the giant faux truffle at the entrance to town
bigger than Big Boy's double-deck hamburger

back home, our only point of comparison,
which meant we had no point. Truffles weren't about
being big. The dogs who dug them up

were peeing on the cathedral. Married four years,
living abroad for the first time, we asked for an *etto*
trusting our Italian measure for meat or cheese.

The man scooped a bunch onto his scale
and promptly asked us to give him
all the money in the world. We coughed. We asked

for two truffles then, and paid the man only half
the world's money. As we drove back over mountains
in a car that had no gear for climbing,

the fumes emerged from the sealed bag.
Married four years. The fumes—
the odor of truffle—I felt like I had just

fucked the earth. Delirious dirt. Lust. Sin.
Sin where money did not matter.
We left them downstairs in the cupboard

then called our friend long distance
in Rome who smelled the truffle
over the phone line and told us

to bury them in rice till we were ready
to use them. The rice sizzled like a snake
in its glass jar as I sunk my truffled hand

down and buried them. Time settled into
its own country. The smell still lingered.
The smell slipped beneath our covers.

Oh, it buried us.

*Sherman Alexie*

# THE ANATOMY OF MUSHROOMS

Now, after all of these years, I remember the woman, whom
    I loved,
who casually mentioned that mushrooms reminded her of
    penises
though I cannot recall for sure if the comparison fascinated or
    repelled her.
Soon after that conversation, she left me for another woman

and though I too have since fallen in love with and married
another woman, I often pause in the middle of lovemaking
to think about the fog-soaked forest into which we all travel
to think about the damp, dank earth in to which we all plunge
    our hands

to search for water and spore and root and loam
to search for water and room and roof and home.

# MUSHROOMS

In this moist season,
mist on the lake and the thunder
afternoons in the distance

they ooze up through the earth
during the night,
like bubbles, like tiny
bright red balloons
filling with water;
a sound below sound, the thumbs of rubber
gloves turned softly inside out.

In the mornings, there is the leafmould
starred with nipples,
with cool white fishgills,
leathery purple brains,
fist-sized suns dulled to the colour of embers,
poisonous moons, pale yellow.

## ii

Where do they come from?

For each thunderstorm that travels
overhead there's another storm
that moves parallel in the ground.
Struck lightning is where they meet.

Underfoot there's a cloud of rootlets,
shed hairs or a bundle of loose threads

blown slowly through the midsoil.
These are their flowers, these fingers
reaching through darkness to the sky,
these eyeblinks
that burst and powder the air with spores.

## iii

They feed in shade, on halfleaves
as they return to water,
on slowly melting logs,
deadwood. They glow
in the dark sometimes. They taste
of rotten meat or cloves
or cooking steak or bruised
lips or new snow.

## iv

It isn't only
for food I hunt them
but for the hunt and because
they smell of death and the waxy
skins of the newborn,
flesh into earth into flesh.

Here is the handful
of shadow I have brought back to you:
this decay, this hope, this mouth-
ful of dirt, this poetry.

# RUIN · COLLAPSE

the mushroom hunters
return empty-handed . . .
fussing

—*Kobayashi Issa*

after the downpour
mushrooms and windfall apples—
summer moon

—*Charles Trumbull*

rouge mushrooms;
in the sleeve the setting sun,
coming back from the hills!

—*Keiko*

*Robert Hass*

# FALL

Amateurs, we gathered mushrooms
near shaggy eucalyptus groves
which smelled of camphor and the fog-soaked earth.
Chanterelles, puffballs, chicken-of-the-woods,
we cooked in wine or butter,
beaten eggs or sour cream,
half expecting to be
killed by a mistake. "Intense perspiration,"
you said late at night,
quoting the terrifying field guide
while we lay tangled in our sheets and heavy limbs,
"is the first symptom of attack."

Friends called our aromatic fungi
"liebestoads" and only ate the ones
that we most certainly survived.
Death shook us more than once
those days and floating back
it felt like life. Earth-wet, slithery,
we drifted toward the names of things.
Spore prints littered our table
like nervous stars. Rotting caps
gave off a musky smell of loam.

*Marvin Bell*

# THE BOOK OF THE DEAD MAN (FUNGI)

> Live as if you were already dead.
> —*Zen admonition*

## 1. *About the Dead Man and Fungi*

The dead man has changed his mind about moss and mold.
About mildew and yeast.
About rust and smut, about soot and ash.
Whereas once he turned from the sour and the decomposed,
      now he breathes deeply in the underbelly of the earth.
Of mushrooms, baker's yeast, fungi of wood decay, and the dogs
      preceding their masters to the burnt acre of morels.
And the little seasonals themselves, stuck on their wobbly pin stems.
For in the pan they float without crisping.
For they are not without a hint of the sublime, nor the curl of a hand.
These are the caps and hairdos, the mini-umbrellas, the zeppelins of a
      world in which human beings are heavy-footed mammoths.
Puffballs and saucers, recurrent, recumbent, they fill the encyclopedia.
Not wrought for the pressed eternity of flowers or butterflies.
Loners and armies alike appearing overnight at the point of return.
They live fast, they die young, they will be back.

## 2. *More About the Dead Man and Fungi*

Fruit of the fungi, a mushroom's birthing is an arrow from below.
It is because of Zeno's Paradox that one cannot get there by half-measures.
It is the fault of having anything else to do.
The dead man prefers the mushroom of the gatherer to that of the farmer.
Gilled or ungilled, stemmed or stemless, woody or leathery, the mushroom
      is secretive, yes, by nature.
Each mushroom was a button, each a flowering, some glow in the dark.

Medicinal or toxic, each was lopped from the stump of eternity.
The dead man has seen them take the shapes of cups and saucers,
of sponges, logs and bird nests.
The dead man probes the shadows, he fingers the crannies and undersides,
he spots the mushroom underfoot just in time.
When the dead man saw a mushrooming cloud above Hiroshima, he knew.
He saw that death was beautiful from afar.
He saw that nature is equidistant from the nourishing and the poisonous,
the good and the bad, the beginning and the end.
He knew the littlest mushroom, shivering on its first day, was a signal.

*Basma Kavanagh*

# TRANSFORMERS

              at the edge
of time sew the dead in white
shrouds that shine with moisture,
with haloes of fine hairs.
They loose the knotted fibres
then knit the dead together,
dissolve their brittle armour,
indifferent to claims
of separate faiths. There are
no chosen people here;
only life trapped in matter.

No one knows what happens
only after, we half-
remember, from the last
time we were dead. They waved
their hands and touched us lightly,
every cell was opened,
all that we were was
weightless, freed to travel
infinitely, born a thousand
times at once from every pore
of earth, shining, armed with nothing.

*Michael Waters*

# MUSHROOMS

*for Mary Oliver*

When the rain touches the rough
　Shoulder of the hill
　　With its makeshift rhythms,

When the rough bowl of the wind
　Offers its leafy porridge,
　　I unleash the retrievers

Along the torn paths in the woods.
　The yellow female leaps over logs
　　Smoldering in their moist beds,

Steaming the air with the tawny odor
　Of mold. The male, black,
　　Plunges through the frost-lit

Recesses of elm, past gallows of oak,
　Faster than the genesis of twilight.
　　As the sky blackens,

Unwinding its canopy of winter stars,
　We pause where the leaves have piled
　　Upon the graves of two settlers,

The clock-maker and his daughter,
　Their dust sifting now
　　Through motes of mildew, perfect

Mushrooms blossoming into October.
No longer traveling, no longer
Foraging the vast forests,

We have gathered here this evening
For a few moments, forever,
To allow the leaves to cradle us

Until the labradors grow restless,
Until the straw basket flames
With the tiny lamps of the dead.

*Simeon Berry*

# THE DOPPELGANGER
# IN THE MUSHROOM FOREST

has difficulty sending back
a dispatch from

the fungal outcroppings.
When it rains, things

get obscene. He stalks
between the chalk

monoliths, one hand
on his double-ought six,

wishing he had validity,
or a vorpal edge. Is this

really what the canon
comes to? Mark Twain

immured behind the white
gills of an amanita,

Dostoevsky a stud
frozen in an isotope

topiary? He's here
to see if what everyone

says about pagination
is true. Keep moving

or someone will
crack wise. *Really?*

*That trauma with that*
*affect? How about*

*something in beige?*
Stand still, and you'll

have to watch
the macrocosm detonate

in the slow, albino
etiquette of decay.

*David Dodd Lee*

# FINDING MUSHROOMS AT DAWN ALONG
## THE PAW PAW RIVER

Dawn unearths them,
naked and blind as grubs
inside their frosted vestments. The underwater gravel
flashes, tongues of alabaster,
while the deer move in two-toed spirals away from center.
And the fish, small coffins,

swim upstream in a blur,
like thoughts, like the ghost
of a print after a man has kissed a woman
on the cheek—a whisper of salt
bathing the tip of his tongue—or the suddenly weightless

drift in the bones
of their hands
as they pick—filling their pockets—the honeycombed
bodies of fruit,
leaving the soft white stems like miniature human ears
behind, in the woods.

*Mary Oliver*

## MUSHROOMS

Rain, and then
the cool pursed
lips of the wind
draw them
out of the ground—
red and yellow skulls
pummeling upward
through leaves,
through grasses,
through sand; astonishing
in their suddenness,
their quietude,
their wetness, they appear
on fall mornings, some
balancing in the earth
on one hoof
packed with poison,
others billowing
chunkily, and delicious—
those who know
walk out to gather, choosing
the benign from flocks
of glitterers, sorcerers,  russulas,
panther caps,
shark-white death angels
in their torn veils
looking innocent as sugar
but full of paralysis:
to eat
is to stagger down

fast as mushrooms themselves
when they are done being perfect
and overnight
slide back under the shining
fields of rain.

*Robert Bly*

## THE MUSHROOM

This white mushroom comes up through the duffy
lith on a granite cliff, in a crack that ice has widened.
The most delicate light tan, it has the texture of a rubber
ball left in the sun too long. To the fingers it feels a
little like the tough heel of a foot.

One split has gone deep into it, dividing it into two
half-spheres, and through the cut one can peek inside,
where the flesh is white and gently naive.

The mushroom has a traveler's face. We know there
are men and women in Old People's Homes whose souls
prepare now for a trip, which will also be a marriage.
There must be travelers all around us supporting us whom
we do not recognize. This granite cliff also travels. Do we
know more about our wife's journey or our dearest friends'
than the journey of this rock? Can we be sure which
traveler will arrive first, or when the wedding will be?
Everything is passing away except the day of this wedding.

## GREEN INSIDE THE DOOR

The summer we lived half-way underground
we watched legs scissor past, until the damp
grass grew to fill our window—wavering,
translucent with green light. Between snarled gibes
about some guy you'd kissed, how poor we were, the rain,
we sat on the couch and stared
into the wettest spring we'd ever seen.
Warm water seeped through walls and drenched the carpet.
We pulled it up and found another world
had thrived in the darkness beneath our feet. It spread.
Exquisite variants of green ran riot,
dappling the walls with almost turquoise spores.
On top of them, starbursts
of black-green blossomed, blackened utter black—
as if mortality crept in each night
and pressed black kisses on the paint.
We scrubbed, waited a night, and they returned.
In bed, not touching, we dreamed they covered us.

At last, we stripped the whole place empty, tossed
shoes, chairs, and knickknacks on the lawn. Our yelling
frightened the neighbors and, hell, it scared us too.
Our red hands smoldered underneath harsh soap.
We fought, and scrubbed possessions till they broke
against the bristles. We left wet shattered things
out drying in the sun, returned
to almost barren rooms that reeked of bleach,
and slept, now holding hands, raw burning hands
that we would not let go. Some books, some chairs,
some knickknacks all survived,
and so did we, my love, but separately.

*Dorianne Laux*

## A CLOSE LOOK

At gravel's edge a small red ball half-buried
in leaf duff. I stoop to pick it up—a dog's
slobbered toy lost in the brush—and discover
the mushroom of my storybook childhood,
squat, red-capped, poisonous, the one suffered
by gnomes in their coned hats and gold-buttoned
livery coats, domed stools they sat on
like doomed drunks in a bar, struggling
not to slide off onto the sawdust floor.
I tip it over with the toe of my shoe, hexes
tumbling from branches bearded with moss,
like crows to something crushed on the road,
and feel the old chill ripple through me as I study
the frilled underside, creamy as custard, vexing
in its deathly fleshiness, part desirable
as a naked thigh, part revolting
as a taloned thrush, black blood caked
along its torn and ruffled lungs.
Part hoax, part wish, invented
by a jealous goddess, precursor to the apple
in its bright rouged skin, its sweet white meat,
the stem a want bone twisting into need, fear
overcome by greed, feeling something like
a pious urge for sin or cruelty, caught
in the netherworld between evil and reprieve:
murderer dressed in a tuxedo, blue egg
harboring the stench of death, the girl fallen
into the granary, her chest filling with gold,
white windowsill lined with yellow mold,
a glowing coal, the icy burn, merciful

ruthlessness, wanting to touch the cold
wound of it, the unblessed that grows
in darkness, the worst of what smells human,
the silken, still born pull of it. I have to
lift my head to catch my breath.

*Lynne Shapiro*

## MUSHROOM FIELDS OF AUTUMN

Stumbling upon them
near the old outhouse after a rain,
more unexpected than flowers,
columns and fluted underbellies rise like
Taj Majals and inverted Eiffel Towers,
architectural wonders that come from the other side
never far from ghostly Indian pipes and beloved ferns,
their ripe colors—silky grey, satin brown,
lustrous sulphur and violet, even—
variegate in the changing light,
enliven the moss and wintergreen
over which they tower for but a day or two,
unforeseen beauty accompanies decline,
begs us not to avert our eyes
from bruises, welts, baroque flourishes of curdle
or symmetry lost to the mouths of animals,
they burst on the scene like grunion running on the beach,
nomadic waxwings crossing my path, always by chance,
there and then gone,
they stand like dunce hats, tiny totems, dancing
teepees, and ancient dolmen.
Don't pluck them! They're not roses, they belong in no vase.
Noiseless do-gooders, they complete their task according to plan.
*Don't trust anyone who doesn't like mushrooms,*
my friend, Luis, whispers, *they are not open.*
*They have not taken in all the possibilities.*

*Kay Ryan*

# WEAKNESS AND DOUBT

Weakness and doubt
are symbionts
famous throughout
the fungal orders,
which admire pallors,
rusts, grey talcums,
the whole palette
of dusts and powders
of the rot kingdom
and do not share
our kind's disgust
at dissolution,
following the
interplay of doubt
and weakness
as a robust
sort of business;
the way we
love construction,
they love hollowing.

*Todd Boss*

## A ROOM OF MUSH

with most porous
roof and softest
soffit, whether on its
pedestal or off it,
tests all our best
notions of what's
structurally sound.

Till it crush or till
it crumble, 'twill
all weather and all
quake withstand,
its gilled and rubber
architecture like
a humble reprimand.

*Mark Halperin*

## MUSHROOMS

*Ex nihilo* or out of thickets, brambles,
  between dead branches, in leaf-piles,
the wild rose that tangles hair, the rope
of vines that trips, their caps poke through.
  Or creamy tan, surrounding you
    like your sex, the blunt slope

and smell of it insistent as a call
  and as deep and unpronounceable,
they pull until you lie down in their bed,
the earth, and night takes you prisoner, shifting,
  shouldering their way through debris, lifting
    the cells of each spongy dream-head.

Charlotte Innes

## CRYPTOBIOTICS

On the surface of desert sand in Utah,
one sees clusters of black specks, a muddy
cushion for lichen to bloom on, or moss,
or, as my friend the philosopher said,

*a sort of subtle bridge between organic*
*and inorganic matter, a fragile world*
*of cryptobiota—dried, dead-looking stuff*
*that's dormant until touched by rainwater . . .*

A bit like the male sex organ, I said,
which, having lost fluid, revives . . . *But only*
*for the briefest span,* he said. *Whereas*
*this soil, ten thousand years in the making,*

*keeps on, a fibrous net of junked bacterial*
*skin that binds the moistened particles*
*together . . .* Unless, I said, careless boots
crush them. But my old friend spoke of dust

and souls, how even dead, our bodies still
conjoin, while I thought, *fibrous net of hair,*
and how the male sex curves under clothes,
making a little cave for slipping fingers in.

*Alison Hawthorne Deming*

# THIS GROUND MADE OF TREES

The giants have fallen.
  I think I can hear the echo
    of their slow composition

the centuries passing
   as note by note
     they fall into the forest's

silent music. Moss has run
   over their backs, mushrooms
     have sprung from the moss,

mold has coated the fungal caps
   and the heartwood
     has given itself to

muffled percussion
   of insect and microbe
     that carpet of sound

that gives the forest its rhythm.
   A nuthatch twits
     or a vole cheeps.

The scent of decay rises
   like steam from a stewpot.
     Anywhere I set my foot

a million lives work
   at metabolizing
     what has gone before them.

The day is shortening
      and the winter wrens have
           something to say about that.

I can almost give thanks
      that the soil will claim me
           but first allow me, dear life,

a few more words of praise
      for this ground made of trees
           where everything is an invitation

to lie down in the moss for good
      and become finally really
           useful, to pull closed

the drapery of lichen
      and let the night birds
           call me home.

# SOURCE ACKNOWLEDGMENTS

Our gratitude goes out to the magazines and books in which some of these poems first appeared.

SHERMAN ALEXIE: "The Anatomy of Mushrooms" reprinted from *One Stick Song.* © 2000 by Sherman Alexie. Reprinted by permission of Hanging Loose Press.

A.R. AMMONS: "I Came in a Dark Woods Upon" and "The Grass Miracles" from *Ommateum: With Doxology.* © 1955, 1983 by A.R. Ammons. Used by permission of W.W. Norton & Company, Inc.

MARGARET ATWOOD: "Mushrooms" from *SELECTED POEMS II: Poems Selected and New, 1976-1986.* © 1987 by Margaret Atwood. Reprinted by permission of Houghton Mifflin Harcourt Publishing Company.

DAVID AXELROD: "Georgic: For My Friends Who Never Find Any," first appeared in the *Southern Poetry Review* (Winter 1996) and was reprinted in their 50th Anniversary anthology, *Don't Leave Hungry* (Arkansas University Press, 2009).

JOHN BARGOWSKI: A version of "7 Precious Mushrooms" first appeared in *West Branch.* Reprinted by permission of the poet.

MARVIN BELL: "The Book of the Dead Man (Fungi)" appeared originally in *Ecotone.* © 2008 by Marvin Bell. Reprinted by permission of the poet.

SIMEON BERRY: "The Doppelganger in the Mushroom Forest" used by permission of the poet.

ELIZABETH BISHOP: "The Shampoo" from *The Complete Poems 1927-1979.* © 1979, 1983 by Alice Helen Methfessel.

ROBERT BLY: "The Mushroom" reprinted from *Reaching Out to the World: New and Selected Prose Poems* (White Pine Press, 2009). © 2009 by Robert Bly. Reprinted by permission of the poet.

TODD BOSS: "A Room of Mush" used by permission of the poet.

JOHN CAGE: excerpts from *Silence* and *A Year from Monday.* © 1962, 1967 by John Cage. Reprinted by permission of Wesleyan University Press.

JIM DANIELS: "Sin With a Little God in It" used by permission of the poet.

ALISON HAWTHORNE DEMING: "This Ground Made of Trees" from *Rope.* © 2009 by Penguin. Reprinted by permission of the poet.

XUE DI: "The Mushroom River" from *Heart Into Soil*, Burning Deck Press, 1998.

ADAM DICKINSON: "The Good" and "Contributions to Geometry: Lichen" from *Kingdom, Phylum*. © 2006 by Brick Books. Reprinted by permission of the poet.

EMILY DICKINSON: "The Elf of Plants" from *The Poems of Emily Dickinson*. © 1955 by Thomas Herbert Johnson.

ALAN DUGAN: "Rising in Fall" *New and Collected Poems*. © 1983 by Ecco. Reprinted by permission of Judith Shahn.

DAVID ALAN FOSTER: "ribbed white canopy . . ." used by permission of the poet.

FERRIS GILLI: "cook's worn-out shoes . . ." first appeared online in the *Shiki Haiku Salon* in 1999. Reprinted by permission of the poet.

HARRY GILONIS: "beefsteak fungus" "oyster fungus" and "fly agaric" from *Forty Fungi*. © 1994 by Coracle Books. Reprinted by permission of Coracle Books.

MARK HALPERIN: "Mushrooms" first appeared in *Crab Creek Review* (Spring/Summer 2001). Reprinted by permission of the poet.

ROBERT HASS: "Fall" first appeared in *Field Guide*. © Yale University Press. Reprinted by permission of Yale University Press.

WILLIAM HEYEN: "Mushroom River" first appeared in *TriQuarterly* and in the author's, *Crazy Horse in Stillness* (BOA Editions, 1996). Reprinted by permission of the poet.

CHRISTOPHER HOWELL: "Letting Things Go" first appeared in *The Gettysburg Review*. Reprinted by permission of the poet.

ANDREW HUDGINS: "Green Inside the Door" from *The Never-Ending* (Houghton Mifflin, 1991). Reprinted by permission of the poet.

CHARLOTTE INNES: "Cryptobiotics" first appeared in *The Pinch* (Fall 2007) and in *Reading Ruskin in Los Angeles* (Finishing Line Press, June 2009). Reprinted by permission of the poet.

LOUIS JENKINS: "Mushroom Hunting" from *North of the Cities*. © 2007 by Will o' the Wisp Books. Reprinted by permission of the poet.

LAURA KASISCHKE: "The World's Largest Living Thing" used by permission of the poet.

# ABOUT THE EDITORS

*Kelly Chadwick* has studied mushrooms intermittently for twenty years during which time they have frequented his dreams and drawn him into the woods. He is a fine wine manager for a beverage distributor and lives in Spokane, Washington with his partner, Renée Roehl.

*Renée Roehl* has been reading, writing, and speaking poetry from the age of 8. She has a MFA in creative writing, is a psycho-spiritual counselor, and a writer-in-residence at an alternative high school in Spokane, Washington, where she lives with her quasi-spouse, Kelly Chadwick, two cats, fish, and her garden. She hopes to add chickens to the mix soon.